Soulful Expressions
On Love And Women
By Lady Di

Dianne M. Hicks

1stBooks – rev. 06/25/01

This book is dedicated to my son Robert, my brothers Myron, Rodrick and C. Duane, sister Karen, and cherished memories of brothers Creighton and Geoffrey.

* * * * * * * *

A special thank you to Jewell Gillespie Holley for editing and encouraging me to keep on keeping on. Your positive attitude will always be an inspiration to me. I appreciate your love and friendship. Thank you Kimberly Williams for the beautiful art work on the cover and your belief in me. Also, thanks to the many friends and relatives who never doubted my ability. This book is for you.

TABLE OF CONTENTS

Introduction vii

SPIRITUAL LOVE

Understanding 3
The Gift 5
Only You 7
For Us To Love 9
My Constant Protector 11
No Regard 13
Circles Of Love 15
The Inheritance 17
Love Is 19
The Voice Of God 21
Patience 23

WOMEN AND FAMILY LOVE

Celebration 27
To The Memory Of My Mother 29
Babies Are For Loving 31
To My Son 33
Black Women Parenting Alone 35
Tables Turn 37
Something Very Wonderful Is 39
Happening To Me 39
Brown Babies, White Mamas 41
Tender Love 43
Reflection 45
Dynamic Black Woman! 47
Love Is All 49
The Lady 51
As I Learn To Love Again 53

PAINFUL LOVE

Is It Possible To Love Again?.. 57
You Of All People!.. 59
Love Meant For Only Me... 61
Memories 63
Do You Ever Think About Me?.. 65
The Elusive Lover.. 67
My Heart Belongs To Someone... 69
At The Roadside Café 69
Actions Speak Louder Than Words... 71
To Trust Again 73
On The Night Before Your Birthday... 75
What's It To You! 77
Just Passing Through... 79

SOULFUL LOVE

"My Brown-Man Special" 83
Becoming One.. 85
Once In A While 87
Changes.. 89
The Manifestation Of True Love... 91
Love And Life.. 93
Him 95
Listening... 97
Instant Attraction 99
Love From The Heart 101
Loving 103
In The Twinkling Of An Eye 105
Loves Invitation... 107
The Love Lesson 109
Love Supreme, Supreme Love 111
Thankfulness... 113

INTRODUCTION

Sometimes we have to personally shake ourselves in order to get back on track in our spiritual growth. We have to get quiet and be still enough to listen to God who is always there for us. He is there to help us rejuvenate ourselves, so that we are able to regain our faith and focus our attention on Him. Through meditation we are able to find out our true path and purpose in life.

SPIRITUAL LOVE

God knows our thoughts before we express them.

UNDERSTANDING

I believe that we were put here on this earth to love another. Love can fix every problem we have, and all people are deserving of this love. God loves us unconditionally, and we in-turn must learn to love one another in the same way. Until we accomplish this, we will continue to have unrest in our world, our land, and our families.

God is our Father and we are His children. He is loving, wise, and understanding. In order for us to accomplish this great mission, we need His help. We cannot do it by ourselves. All we need to do is ask.

I want to learn how to give love unconditionally,
and how to accept love graciously.

THE GIFT

The gift
    of caring
    of sharing
    of being

gathered with love
    for men
    for women
    for children

wrapped with kindness,
ribbon tied with gratitude,
and given whenever possible.

Your love encourages me to be strong,
   To be more than I ever thought possible,
   To be full of expectations,
   To be full of vitality,
   Because of you, God
   I can.

ONLY YOU

Only You can make my life complete,
Only You can my desires keep,
Only You can bring about a change,
Only You, my God.

Only You can dry my weeping eyes,
Only You can make a Robin fly,
Only You can make me smile again,
Only You, my God.

Only You can take away the pain,
Only You can encourage me to live again,
Only You can fill my heart with love,
Only You, my God.

The richest blessings come from God.

FOR US TO LOVE

For me

    to be

    might take a lot you see.

For you

    to know

    might take a lot to show you how I feel.

For them

    to guess

    might take a lot to bless us with their prayers.

For God

    to bless

    might take a lot of love for us to share.

Today offers great opportunities. I am to be open,
flexible, and flow with life.

MY CONSTANT PROTECTOR

My life is enriched because of you.
You, love me
Just as I am.

If I am naked, you clothe me.
If I am hungry, you feed me.
If I am weeping, you dry my tears.
If I am praying, you listen.
If my burden is too heavy, you take it.

You, who cared about me before I cared about myself.
You, who taught others to care about me.
You, who taught me to care.
You, who taught me to strive for what is right.
You, who gave me courage and strength.
You are my constant companion.
You are the dearest person to me.
You, my Lord and Savior Jesus Christ.

I owe you everything.

I want to know how to love unconditionally and
accept love graciously.

NO REGARD

To have no regard for others
    hurting them beyond repair,
Is the saddest of all human beings
    for they cannot love and share.

But maybe God will touch their hearts
    giving them a second chance to mend
Other hearts that have been broken,
    other hearts that have been dimmed.

Help me to stand tall and be patient for answers to unanswered prayers.

CIRCLES OF LOVE

Love makes the world go around.

And the world goes around in a circle.

That means when you radiate love,
    love circles right back to you.

Circles of love will surround you and
    make you feel protected and safe.

If God is truly in charge of our lives, we must learn to
look and listen for His signs.

THE INHERITANCE

There is more to being black then

   meets the eye.

There is quality,

A substance,

A love,

An attitude that is inherited

   through the soul.

Your love feels like a wool glove. Snug and warm.

LOVE IS

Love is precious,

Love is gold,

Love is best,

When love is old.

What is happening to my faith if my belief fails
the minute things don't go my way.

THE VOICE OF GOD

Sometimes in my quiet moments
When I kneel down to pray.
I listen to the voice of God
To hear just what He says.

He tells me how to live my life,
The things that I should do,
And even if I don't agree
He tells me things that are true.

Sometimes I need a scolding,
When I've done some wrongful thing,
And He gently calls me back to Him
To bless me just the same.

I know that He still loves me,
Because He tells me so,
And if I listen to Him,
He'll bless me more, you know.

So when you're kneeling quietly
To make known all your cares,
Just take an extra moment
To hear the things He'll share.

Patience is a true test of our love.

PATIENCE

Patience is a virtue that few have,
A virtue that most of us must acquire.
We all must take the test in the game of life.
We must prove our worth.
We must stand erect.
We must have guidance.

Alone we cannot be strong,
Alone we cannot stand firm.
Alone we cannot be.
We must depend on God.

Dianne M. Hicks

WOMEN AND FAMILY LOVE

You are entitled to be proud of who you are.

CELEBRATION

What do I have to celebrate?

What do I have to be joyful about?

So many wonderful things.

My life.

My son.

My blackness, who I am and what I stand for.

The fact that I am.

The fact that my forefathers fought and survived

    whatever they had to in order that I might live today.

What a wonderful creation life is.

That I today can Celebrate!

Mother love is next to God love.

TO THE MEMORY OF MY MOTHER

I remember
   her smile,
   her sharing and caring for us kids.

So much of her was in our home,
   sewing, canning, cleaning.

Special Christmases.

Stretching a dollar,
   not always living her life to its fullest.

Being a mother.
Meeting the demands of seven children.

A special person whose name was Sybil.
Such a beautiful name – Prophetess.

One who foretells the future.
Regal authority.

Yet, no throne to sit upon,
No jewels, riches or crown.

Only a few years snuffed out too soon,
   by struggles, disappointments, illness.

Gone before WE realized a full life with her.

Not knowing her grandchildren,
Beautiful grandchildren.

They would have loved her.
She would have loved them.
There would be so much to share,
   and yet, it will never be.
The lonely years without her have
   been hard.

However, as I remember
   her laughter, her tears,
   her poems, her etchings,
She was a fashion designer.

May our souls meet in eternity.
May we embrace each other,
   and hold each other tight,
   and cry, and kiss,
   and whisper "I love you"
   once again.

I owe so much of who I am to her.

Innocent love is the purest love of all.

BABIES ARE FOR LOVING

Babies are for loving,
Eyes so shiny bright,
Full of smiles and laughter,
To life a sheer delight.

Babies are for kissing,
Squeeze them like a cuddly doll,
Cooing sounds of understanding,
Knowing mother's love.

God touches my heart to help me to do all that's
put before me to do regardless of the circumstances.

TO MY SON

I just called to say I love you,
And hear your sweet voice on the other side.
Coupled with gladness and mystic pleasure,
I hope to hear a glimpse of joy in the voice
I cannot see.

My love for you goes deeper than you can ever know.
And even though my flesh has not touched yours lately,
Never forget my warm kisses of affection
    upon your cheek,
Never forget my tender hugs of comfort,
You experienced so many Moons before.

I love you, my precious bronze baby boy–turned man.

Yesterday, today, tomorrow and always.

Help me to remember to sow my seeds on good ground
where they can take root.

BLACK WOMEN PARENTING ALONE

Black women with children, by themselves–alone

coping,
hoping,
dreaming.

Bearing what life dribbles out to them

always coping,
always hoping,
always dreaming.

For another tomorrow when life will be brighter
       offering new ways

to cope,
to hope,
to dream.

Knowing that if they endure despite difficulties,
       it will be worth

the coping,
the hoping,
the dreaming.

For the future of their offspring so they too can

cope,
hope,
and dream.

Because we can't see the full picture, we sometimes fail
to believe the big picture really exists.

TABLES TURN

I feel
I cry
I laugh.

I need
I want
I desire.

Well meaning people often think of me as some
    superwoman lacking these common emotions.

I work hard because I must.

I set goals that will one day become a reality–
    not just a vision.

Don't trod on my being thinking things will always be
    the same with me; thinking things will always be the
    same with you.

Tables turn.

Today offers miracles we are not aware of.
When we do what God puts before us to do,
miracles can happen.

SOMETHING VERY WONDERFUL IS
HAPPENING TO ME

It will be so wonderful I will think it's a miracle.
I love life and I love miracles and I give thanks.

Things that are wonderful for my eyes to see,
For fantastic miracles are happening to me!

Positive thoughts send miracles to me.
Wonderful miracles flowing free,
Something very wonderful is happening to me!

The way things look to our naked eye is not always how they appear. In fact, most of the time our vision is clouded by our experiences of the past.

BROWN BABIES, WHITE MAMAS

Have you ever wondered about brown babies with white
mamas?

I have often watched our brown babies with their white mamas.

Watched

their gestures,
their nurturing,
their love.

The care white mamas seem to have for their young.

Listen white mama,
I pray you love your brown babies

enough to quiet their fears when they have haunting dreams,
enough to kiss away their pain when the world inflicts hurt,
enough to keep them positive and optimistic for the future,
enough to let them know that because they are your brown
babies,

together you can make a difference.

A mother's love is steadfast.

TENDER LOVE

Tender is a baby's love,
Remember, you're all he's got,

    for eating,
    for walking,
    for talking and such.

Tender are your baby's hugs
And likewise yours to him,

    for soothing,
    for cuddling,
    for loving and such.

Being positive assures me of the goodness that is already mine. Dear God, help me to stay positive.

REFLECTION

Mellow is my mood as I lazily recline while listening
    to the indigenous sounds of jazz.

Lying here brings back memories of an early love.

A love when flesh was innocent and searching,

Wishing and hoping the future offered undeserved riches
    that could be enjoyed then.

However, as I reflect on yesterdays, I now know that to
    live life to its fullest takes

    lots of prayer,
    lots of faith,
    lots of forgiveness,
    lots of love,

Not only from others, but from myself.

Never giving up the dream to hope,

Always being positive so that the link between my
    generation and the next will continue.

Always give the best that you have to offer.

DYNAMIC BLACK WOMAN!

Dynamic black woman!
With your skin of many hues,
Smooth as silk,
High cheek bones,
Exuding royalty from which you've come.

Dynamic black woman!
Wearing garments of vibrant colors,
Displaying your uniqueness,
Your gift and talent for artistic flair.

Dynamic black woman!

Educated and courageous enough to
    make it on your own.

Graceful enough to blend with that
    special man of your choice.

Religious enough to become a pillar
    of strength for both of you.

Sensitive enough to demonstrate love
    and compassion to your children.

Humble enough to pray to God for
    guidance and support.

And through it all,

Faithful enough to know that despite the
    struggle, love conquers all that can
    ever exist.

The tapestry of my life is woven into a delicate pattern of faith and love. God is the Master Weaver who has woven every thread for my benefit.

LOVE IS ALL

Love is grateful,
Love is peace,
Love is joy,
Love is bliss.

Love is serene,
Love is caring,
Love is wisdom,
Love is sharing.

Love is for friends,
And family too,
Love is for me,
Love is for you.

Sometimes we have to rely on the vision within.

THE LADY

I watched her cross the street.
Her steps shaky and unsure,
However, she crossed it just the same.
She went forward down the street
Towards her destination,
Past my office window.

The leash in hand
A leash to life,
To freedom,
To be.

Freedom to live a fuller life,
Freedom to work,
Freedom to play,
Freedom to envision the world.

You see,
Her freedom lies in his eyes.
Her friend and constant companion.
Her God–Friend.
Her dog.

Once again, I am humbled.
Thank you God,
For all that I have.

God expects us to learn to love again because
we are created from love.

AS I LEARN TO LOVE AGAIN

As I learn to love again, I will strive
to show others that I care.

As I learn to love again, I will be more open
to communication.

As I learn to love again, I will work on being
more attentive and cooperative.

As I learn to love again, I will give without
expecting in return.

As I learn to love again, I will listen without
judging first.

As I learn to love again, I will be more prayerful.

As I learn to love again, I will express my
feelings so that others can recognize them.

As I learn to love again, I will be open to
sharing myself more.

As I learn to love again, I will learn to overcome
fears of rejection.

As I learn to love again, I will be understanding
and supportive.

As I learn to love again, I will learn to forgive
others as well as myself.

As I learn to love again, I will learn to make
wiser choices.

As I learn to love again, half the fun of loving
is learning to love more.

As I learn to love again, I smile, relax and trust
again in God's all knowing power.

Dianne M. Hicks

PAINFUL LOVE

Help me dear God to find my way to love again.

IS IT POSSIBLE TO LOVE AGAIN?

Is it possible to love again,
    and be vulnerable once more?

Is it possible to love again,
    without the keeping score?

Of who was right,
    and who was wrong,
    of who was weak,
    and who was strong,
    to open up and not be hurt.

I must believe and hope again
    that love can have another chance.

That I can smile and laugh again
    that this time love can last.

Making me feel free again
    to love and feel secure.

Where I can truly be myself
    without the enemy of fear.

Yes, I can
    because loves lives wherever I am!

Sometimes we know better, but we don't listen to God.

YOU OF ALL PEOPLE!

You of all people!
Had the audacity to come,
And awaken my body once more,
Entering my heart, mind and soul
After a long hiatus.

You of all people!
Had the audacity to come,
Teasing my earlobes,
Dancing with my lips and hips,
Letting me taste your breath again.

You of all people!
Had the audacity to come,
Devouring me like a delicious plum,
Expecting me to succumb,
If only for a brief moment.

You of all people!
Had the audacity to come.
But I of all people,
Had the audacity to accept!
And I KNEW better!!!

The strength of the Lord is with me. I will fear nothing and no one.

LOVE MEANT FOR ONLY ME

What does it take to have love that's sweet,
To have love that's endless as eternity,
To have love that's so blind no one can see?
What does it take to have love that's meant
    for only me?

What does it take to have eyes that shine,
To have a smile with timeless lines meant for me,
To have a love vision seen beyond the sea?
What does it take to have love that's meant
    for only me?

Oh, I have a mate who says he cares,
Who lives in a house that he and I share.
We sleep together in a saddened bed.
Who says he loves me, but not a tear he sheds.

I have waited long for the one that will be,
By my side constantly,
But the way is long and often lonely,
As I wait for the love that's meant for me only.

Thank you for today God. I am feeling great!
I love you and I know you love me.

MEMORIES

The echo of his laughter still rings softly in my ears,

Plans that hinted of tomorrows,

Plans I knew were clear.

How I loved that man so deeply,

No one else could enter in,

My thoughts were his completely,

My love could be his again.

However, as I move on toward the future,

Brighter days will soon be here.

Days of tender, gentle, love strokes,

From a lover who will care.

Our vision is clouded. However, when we take God
as our partner, our vision becomes lucid.
He directs our path.

DO YOU EVER THINK ABOUT ME?

Do you ever think about me
When you go to bed at night?
Of the times we spent together,
Of the love we thought was right,
Of the promises we sanctioned
Vowing never to depart.
Do you ever think about me?
Am I still part of your heart?

Do you ever think about me?
Letting go was hard to do.
Often memories of sweetness
Stir my heart strings of you.
Knowing you still cared a little
Would help me somehow to dream.
Do you ever think about me?
Do you know just what I mean?

Caring for you made me realize
Love can grow from a small flame,
For my love kept growing stronger,
But yours somehow had waned.
But as I lay here on my pillow,
With my eyes tear-stained and sore,
Do you ever think about me?
Can you love me just once more?

You deserve so much more than you're getting.

THE ELUSIVE LOVER

The elusive lover.

Just when I get accustomed to you,
    you're gone again.

Somehow I thought, this time, I made a difference.
Somehow I thought, this time, you cared.
Somehow I thought, this time, your feelings
    were sincere.

Perhaps not.

Hearts deserve to be happy,

    loving,

    forgiving,

    uncomplicated,

    serene,

    entwined,

    forever.

Just when I get accustomed to you,
    you're gone again.

The Sun does shine in the morning. Help me, God to know that you are planning only good for me – no matter what appears to be.

MY HEART BELONGS TO SOMEONE
AT THE ROADSIDE CAFÉ

He'd come into the café,
He was handsome, big and tall.
He'd sit and order coffee,
He wouldn't smile at all.

One day our eyes made contact,
My breath caught in my throat.
I kept on serving people,
Doing all my tasks by rote.

Before he left the café,
He came and whispered in my ear,
That if I was free by seven,
He'd meet me then back here.

As I looked up in those big brown eyes,
My heart melted on the spot.
I nodded yes, like a star-struck dove,
That was the beginning of our love.

We met each other right on time,
Just like we said we would.
I loved him from the very start,
I knew together, we'd be good!

But his heart was not for me to have,
The thrill was gone too soon.
The next month he was with another,
On the far side of the room.

He winked just like I still was his,
I turned my head away.
How could my heart belong to him
At this roadside café?

But as I end this story,
I'm still trying to be brave,
Because my heart still longs,
For someone at the roadside café.

Dianne M. Hicks

Continual prayer encourages me to make right choices.

ACTIONS SPEAK LOUDER THAN WORDS

You say that you love me with all of your heart,
You say that we will never part,
The way you're acting, I think it's absurd,
Actions, speak louder than words.

You say that you can't wait to hold me tight,
You say that you can't wait to kiss me each night.
I feel our relationship is not secure,
Actions, speak louder than words.

It seems you and I have so little to say,
Our interests are going separate ways,
But to have you whisper in my ear and hold me tight,
Would be such a welcomed delight.

But what's happening now is plain to see,
That you don't really care about me.
You say that's not true.
Can I believe you?
Actions, speak louder than words!

Now is the time for change. What could it be?
Now is the time to shift my gears, to grow,
to see, to be me.

TO TRUST AGAIN

To trust again is not an easy thing to do,
For we guard our feelings with a shield of defensive
    behavior.
Walls and fences surround our feelings and protect
    them from outside influences.

We fear the unknown.

To trust again is not an easy thing to do.
We stick with the familiar not wanting to make changes.
Wearing our true feelings once again takes courage,
And sometimes we feel rather frail,
But God is near to help us try.

I go forward knowing all of my requests are being met.
God blesses my life continually and I give thanks.

ON THE NIGHT BEFORE YOUR BIRTHDAY

On the night before your birthday,
I sit by the open fire
With a heart that longs for you,
Spilling over with desire.

What could you be doing?
Did you leave a clue?
Are you thinking of me?
Are you being true?

All our happy times together
Have been great, but now I'm blue
On the night before your birthday,
Here I sit, waiting for you.

Candle lit dinner on the table,
You see, I had it all prepared,
Had the champagne chilled and waiting,
Even had homemade baked bread.

But you haven't come to eat it,
No, I haven't hear a word,
This night before your birthday
My tear stained cheeks and eyes are blurred.

So this night before your birthday,
I sit here all alone.
Presents wrapped in colored ribbon,
Wait for your surprised return.

Though I haven't had a phone call,
I'll wait here optimistically,
On the night before your birthday,
I pray, you come home to me.

Love is powerful. It can change who you are.

WHAT'S IT TO YOU!

What's it to you
    what I think,
When I put
    my words in ink.

What's it to you
    how I feel,
When you knew
    my love was real.

What's it to you
    at this time,
When you know
    our love won't shine.

Well I'll venture
    just to say,
We've already
    had our day.

Knowing all our
    love has passed,
And it's sad
    it didn't last.

Knowing deep within
    you cared,
Help my feelings
    to be spared.

And in the future days
    when my heart's no longer swayed,
I'll smile upon the hour
    when love had me in your power.

Real love doesn't hurt. Thank you God, I'm learning.

JUST PASSING THROUGH

Could it be
    you were just passing through?

I looked,
    and you were there.

I looked again
    and you were gone.

Gone
    to God knows where.

From someone I know
    to someone I knew,
    the time was oh, so brief.

Someone I tried to feel close to,
    but who didn't feel close to me.

For you didn't think much of my feelings,
    despite what I felt for you.

However, time will heal my heart,
    and take away my pain.

And guess what?

Someday,

I won't even remember your name.

Dianne M. Hicks

SOULFUL LOVE

Who's that special man in your life?

"MY BROWN-MAN SPECIAL"

My Brown-Man special,
   oh, he's my kind of guy,
   who's proud when he struts,
   with a gleam in his eye.

Why he's all that a woman
   could want and more
   and everyone turns their head
   when he walks through a door.

Oh, he's my Brown-Man special
   with a twink in his eyes,
   with a smile on his lips,
   and his feeling of pride.

Oh, he's caring and sweet,
   he's a family man too,
   a sportsman is he,
   and he's honest and true.

He's my Brown-Man special,
   he knows what he's about,
   doesn't have to say nothing,
   doesn't have to shout.

Oh he's sure of his talk,
   you can believe what he says,
   not a frivolous thinker,
   but a man that's well read.

He's my Brown-Man special,
   and in love he's the king,
   his touch and his kisses,
   can make my heart sing.

My Brown-Man special
   is for nobody but me,
   no, you can't have him sistah!
   so don't get happy with glee.

Get your own man,
   the world's full you know.
   cause this man is mine,
   and he's only for show!

Dianne M. Hicks

In uniting we become one.

BECOMING ONE

Open up your heart to me
So I can see,
The nature of your beauty,
The radiance of your soul.

I in-turn will open up myself
To Thee.
My soul entwines with yours.
We are one.

Thank you for today God. I love you and
I know you love me.

ONCE IN A WHILE

Once in a while
    I remember you.
Good times together
    when our hearts were true.

What has happened to the years gone by?
The dreams we shared that would never die.
Circumstances changed our lives,
    our hearts.
We both have found someone new.

But once in a while, I remember you.

God wants only the best for us, and if we are obedient
and always put Him first, the best can be ours.

CHANGES

When we were young,
Your hair was fair,
Your eyes they sparkled bright.
Your body built in every way,
You were such a delight.

But what has happened through the years?
You've changed in every way.
I hardly recognized you there,
Much to my dismay.

Your hair is thin,
Your eyes are sad,
How has life been to you?
It hurts to think that life can treat
    some kind and some so cruel.

One never knows what lies ahead.
It's never what you think.
And yet we all have had to take the
    bitter with the sweet.

But blessed are they, who still can say,
Why I've changed for the better.
But be kind to those who've crossed your path
    that life has been so bitter.

True love is a precious experience that we all want.
It is important to let God know our desires. It is
equally important to let God guide us.

THE MANIFESTATION OF TRUE LOVE

We go along from day to day
And before we know it,
In the twinkling of an eye,
Dormant feelings blossom into love.

It's hard to imagine life before the manifestation of love.

True love.

Love that is a consuming passion.
Love that grips our very souls,
Taking us to foreign heights we have never been before.

This love experience is unique!

A different time,
A different place,
A different feeling.

We are soul mates.

True love is sanctioned by God who loves us very much.

LOVE AND LIFE

All that I am encompasses all that I am meant to be.

Whatever I am is already deep within me waiting to
     be shared.

I am loved.
I am loving.

I give because I desire to.
I live because I love life.

A gift from God.

I savor each moment of life like a delicious flavor
     I want to cling to when eating a favorite food.

Ah, the taste is magnificent!

Sometimes God sends us a friend that makes us feel
special and that's okay.

HIM

A whisper so soft you have to strain to
    hear it.
A kiss that means he's yours.
You hold hands and look into each other's eyes
    as if to look away would change the world.
A heart that skips a beat, throughout the day,
    just thinking of his name.
A feeling so deep that it would take seas to
    erase.
A breath cut short because suddenly you
    remember how he held your hand last night.
A voice that makes the blood rush through
    your entire being.
A thought, he said he would be by this evening,
And time, you cannot wait until he's in your
    presence once again.

Today offers great opportunities. I am to be open,
flexible, and flow with life.

LISTENING

I'm listening to my heart,
To hear what it says.
My soul is tuned in,
To the music it plays.

I'm listening to my heart,
It is pounding of love,
Rare words of encouragement,
Come from above.

I'm listening to my heart,
My true love is near,
As I tune into thoughts,
That I'm ready to hear.

As I give love, love is returned.

INSTANT ATTRACTION

You looked at me.

I looked at you.

We both knew,

that something more could be between us.

We smiled.

We chatted.

We danced.

Instantly, we were at a point of no return.

I am grateful for every gift of love that I can share.

LOVE FROM THE HEART

I have a grateful heart,
With kindness to impart,
For I will gladly do,
Most anything for you.

To have a cheerful smile,
I'd walk that extra mile,
To share all that I might,
I'd comfort you tonight.

Help me to know and be,
All that I could with Thee,
For you I'd give my all,
Just call.

To love and be loved is an extraordinary gift
from God.

LOVING

We could be a synchronized pair,

Our love could cross boundaries rare,

Love that with sparks would fly,

Love that would never die,

You and I.

We could jet across the sky,

Scale Mount Everest on high,

Like lovebirds entwined we'd be,

Me loving you, you loving me,

You and I.

Passionate love is deep within waiting to surface.

IN THE TWINKLING OF AN EYE

We go along from day to day,
And before we know it,
In the twinkling of an eye,
Dormant feelings turn into love.

It's hard to imagine
life before love.

True love.

Love that is a consuming passion,
Love that grips our very souls,
Taking us to foreign heights
We have never known before.

There is an invitation to love someone everyday.

LOVE'S INVITATION

Love invites me in and I accept.

Love pulls up a chair for me and I sit.

Love serves me a delicious meal and I am full.

Love asks me to stay, so I linger.

And as I do,

I discover,

That without love in my life,

I have not lived.

I no longer want to face living alone.

I must commit.

And if I take love as a partner,

I cannot half step.

I must go all the way.

Help me to wear a glow of radiance and a tone
of love. I give love and I accept love.

THE LOVE LESSON

Give love to someone near and far,
Give love because you care,
Give love, it is a precious gift,
A wholesome treasure rare.

Most people want love in their lives,
To give is to receive.
Mistaken we look everywhere,
Even in our dreams.

Love has to come from you and me,
It must be given unconditionally.
The lesson is to give all you can,
That is God's perfect plan.

The best kind of love is committed love.

LOVE SUPREME, SUPREME LOVE

The enchanting power of being in love,

Uniting you together as one,

Committing the love of your souls,

Making you whole to experience that
    infinite space that too few have known.

This means not giving up,

But trying to make what you have work
    for both of you,

Because you two have an invested
    interest–each other.

And once you reach a point of no return,

Less will never be good enough.

Your choice, of course, is to stay forever.

THANKFULNESS

I give thanks for all I can write, share and be.
I give thanks dear Lord God, to Thee.

www.ingramcontent.com/pod-product-compliance
Lightning Source LLC
Chambersburg PA
CBHW052246290526
45785CB00016B/1405